CW00520413

Basketball is Psychology presents

THE ART OF EMBRACING ADVERSITY

A GUIDE TO LIVING A MEANINGFUL LIFE IN THE MIDST OF LOSSES, SETBACKS, AND UNCERTAINTY

2nd EDITION

BasketballisPsychology.com

Written by Julie Fournier

Edited by Abbey Cruzes

Cover art by Graham Fournier

To Kobe,

My hero. My role model. My inspiration.

Your work ethic, your passion, and your relentless pursuit of excellence were unmatched.

Most of all, your focus on the mental side of the game is what inspired Basketball is Psychology. I'll make sure your legacy lives on and your mentality gets passed down to the next generation.

You are my muse.

Rest in peace, Kobe.

I wrote this book because I needed to read it.

Three weeks after the first edition of *The Art of Embracing Adversity* was published, I broke my hand. I would wake up every morning with no motivation to get out of bed, and later I would cry myself to sleep. Wasn't I supposed to know how to deal with this? Wasn't I supposed to be okay? But I didn't know how to deal with it, and I wasn't okay. Things didn't get better until I made peace with the fact that it was okay that I wasn't okay. It was then that I realized this book was far from finished.

In the first edition, I failed to acknowledge that when you first encounter adversity, you probably won't be okay, and that is okay. It's better to hold the weight of those emotions than to hide from them. The first step to healing is grieving. My hope is that whether you're injured, burnt out, discouraged, or heartbroken (I was all four), I hope this book will help you grow through it. This book is a compilation of things that have helped me feel seen, encouraged, and inspired when I was at my lowest. I wrote it primarily for injured basketball players, but the principles apply to anyone going through a hard time. Embracing adversity will look different for everyone; it's an art, not a science.

Introduction

"If you're alive, there's a purpose for your life."
-   Rick Warren

According to *Psychology Today*, the average high school kid has the same level of anxiety as the average psychiatric patient in the early 1950's. This is the most depressed, anxious, and lonely generation yet; and that was even before 2020.

There are endless amounts of diets out there: vegan, vegetarian, keto, low fat, gluten-free, dairy-free, organic, paleo, intermittent fasting, etc... Some are putting butter in coffee when a decade ago, everyone avoided butter at all costs. Fruits used to be the clear choice for a healthy snack, now they are too high in sugar.

Needless to say, it's confusing. If it's that confusing understanding what it takes to be healthy *physically*, how much more confusing is it to understand what it takes to be healthy *mentally*?

As athletes, we see trainers for strength, conditioning, and skill training several times a week. We see doctors and dentists on a regular basis. We prepare our bodies meticulously. We watch what we eat, how much water and electrolytes we drink, and how much rest we get. We stretch, we foam roll, and we take ice baths, but so often we neglect our most important asset: our mind.

If an athlete rolls their ankle in practice, they follow the protocol: tell the coach, go see the trainer who might refer them to a doctor. There is no stigma around physical injuries. Athletes don't feel shame for needing professional help to get back to 100%.

If an athlete feels severely depressed, only one in five will seek help. Why? There's a stigma around needing help to get our minds healthy. The world of athletics has taught us to equate showing emotion with weakness, thus equating a face of stone with strength.

The problem is, athletes suffer from mental illness at a much higher rate than those outside of athletics. One in five people are currently struggling with a mental illness. For athletes, that number is one in three; or at least it *was,* then 2020 happened and things got much worse.

In a study led by UW Health Researcher Dr. Tim McGuine, with the objective to identify, "How Covid-19 related school closures and sport cancellations in Wisconsin have impacted the health of adolescent athletes," findings show the mental health of athletes has taken a toll in 2020.

- 65% reported anxiety symptoms
- 25% are suffering from moderate to severe anxiety
- The rate of mild to severe depression jumped from 31% to 68%
- Physical activity was down 50%

We can hop on a scale, look in the mirror, or go through a workout to see if our physical health is doing well. With mental health, it's a lot harder to measure. With a mental illness, you could be in the worst pain you have ever felt in your life and you could still look completely normal to the outside world.

In 2020, everyone was talking about regulations and precautions for going back to school and restarting athletics in the midst of the pandemic. Everyone was talking about when the season would start, how we would social distance, disinfect, and prevent the spread. Lots of problems came to light in the pandemic, but no one was talking about athletes' mental health.

For most athletes, playing the game is their source of joy. Their teammates are like their family. For a lot of athletes, sports are an escape, it's how they cope when they're stressed. With little to no warning, all of that was taken.

So now how do we cope? How do we make sense of this adversity we are facing? We were already living in the most depressed, anxious, and lonely generation before a global pandemic intensified these problems.

In the midst of all this adversity, how do you stay mentally healthy? How do you find joy? There is nothing more important than your mental health, and the purpose of this book is to help guide your thoughts in the midst of setbacks, difficulties, pandemics, and injuries.

You Matter

If you take nothing else from this book, I want you to take these two words: *you matter.*

You matter to this world, you matter to people, and you matter to history. You have infinite value. The world needs you. You are not an accident. You have a purpose. Any voice telling you otherwise is lying, don't listen to it.

You were put on this earth for a reason. You are not here only to survive, you are here to make a difference. You were designed to live a life of significance. You were designed with a unique set of dreams, gifts, and passions, and the world needs you to use them. You are amazing, don't you dare waste it. The world doesn't need a mediocre, lesser version of you. The world needs the best version of you. As long as you are still on this planet, you have work to do, a great story to live out, and a purpose to fulfill.

I believe you are capable of great things, and you are unstoppable; because even though you are facing setbacks, failure, doubt, and adversity, you continue pushing through it all. Not only do you keep going, but you also *thrive* in adversity.

My hope is that this book will help you realize your potential and live into it. I want this book to help you use adversity to launch you into greatness. I don't want you to simply get through, avoid, or overcome adversity, I want you to embrace it because I believe you will be better on the strength of it.

Some people get hit with adversity and they crumble. They throw pity parties, spend all their time feeling sorry for themselves, get stuck, and get bitter. They get discouraged and quit when life gets hard. They let a few difficult chapters in their story ruin their lives. Don't you dare let that be your life story. Your story is different. In your story, you *do not* let adversity distract you. Instead, you use the adversity to shape your character into a stronger, more empathetic version of yourself. You matter, and your story matters. Make sure you are telling a good one.

Chapter 1

Hero or

Victim?

"Everything can be taken from man
but one thing: the last of human
freedoms–to choose one's attitude
in any given set of circumstances."
- Dr. Viktor Frankl

According to author Donald Miller, there are four characters in every story, "The victim is the character who feels like they have no way out. The villain is the character who makes others small. The hero is the character who faces their challenges and transforms. The guide is the character who helps the hero."

These characters exist in stories because they exist in real life. At any given moment of our lives, we can play any of these characters. When a friend needs advice, we usually play the guide. When we want revenge, we play the villain. When we feel helpless, we play the victim. When we have the opportunity to overcome a challenge, we play the hero.

Tyler Jones once said, "At the end of the day, your life is just a story. If you don't like the direction it's going, change it. Rewrite it. When you rewrite a sentence, you erase it and start over until you get it right. Yes, it's a little more complicated with a life, but the principle is the same. And remember, don't let anyone ever tell you that your revisions are not the truth."

If your life is a story, then before you decide what your story will be about or where your story is going, you have to decide which character you will play in the story. Will you play the hero or will you play the victim?

What if your problem is not your circumstances, what if your problem is how you view yourself?

When faced with adversity, most people choose to view themselves as the victim. Victims play a small part in the story. They have no way to take action and advance the story.

Now, there are real victims who are truly helpless and do need to be rescued, but more often than not, you do not need to dwell in the victim mentality.

When challenges arise, you have a choice: view yourself as the victim or view yourself as the hero.

The difference between a hero and a victim is that when they encounter hardship, the hero takes action, rises to the occasion, and transforms into a better version of themselves, while the victim does not take action and waits to be rescued.

Adversity is your boll weevil.

In the town of Enterprise, Alabama, there is a boll weevil monument. Boll weevils are pesky beetles known for destroying cotton. In the early 1900's, the town of Enterprise, Alabama had its cotton crop devastated by the boll weevils. The economy of the small town was quickly spiraling downward thanks to the boll weevils.

One farmer, however, was in a lot of debt. He could not afford another season of the boll weevils destroying his cotton.

At this point, the farmer had a choice: he could play the victim and give up on farming (after all, the boll weevils had destroyed his crops year after year) or he could play the hero and advance the story by trying something new.

His banker told him he should try planting peanuts. So he played the hero and planted peanuts. As a result, he had a great year. He did so well, everyone else in the town started planting peanuts. In 1917, Coffee County sold over 5 million dollars worth of peanuts. By 1919, they were the largest peanut-producing county in the United States. The economy in Enterprise was thriving. The entire town was so grateful that their economy had been saved; thanks to the boll weevils.

But why build a boll weevil monument? For years the boll weevils had destroyed so much cotton and cost the farmers lots of money. If it was not for the boll weevils, the farmers would have never gone looking for a better cash crop. Thanks to the boll weevils, the farmers were doing better than ever. The adverse situation made them re-evaluate and find a better way to do things. Without the boll weevils, Enterprise would have stayed a mediocre cotton-producing town. Had the man in debt played the victim, they wouldn't be the largest peanut-producing county in the United States. *The boll weevils were the best thing that could have possibly happened.*

Adversity is your boll weevil. What if, by choosing to view yourself as a hero, the adverse situation you are facing will lead you to discover and become a better version of yourself? When you start looking at adversity from this perspective, you won't want to hide from it, you'll want to build a monument out of appreciation for it.

"Victorious is the person who knows how to make stepping stones out of stumbling stones."
- John C. Maxwell

The truth is that heroes and victims are often up against the same thing, only how they view themselves is different. The hero believes he can become a better version of himself to overcome the challenge. The victim believes they don't stand a chance against the challenge so they remain idle and don't rise to the challenge.

Your locus of control is the mechanism in you that decides how much responsibility you take for your life.

The difference between a hero and a victim is their locus of control. The hero has a high internal locus of control, while the victim has a high external locus of control.

You can tell someone has a high external locus of control because they believe that when life gets hard, it's because of something outside of them and they can't do anything about it. They don't believe they are the authors of their own life stories.

You can tell when someone has a high internal locus of control, when life gets hard, they take responsibility for doing something about it because they believe that they are in charge of their life. If they don't like where their life is headed, they believe they can grab the pen and author a better story into existence.

A victim mindset is often an excuse. Viewing yourself as the victim excuses you from taking responsibility for being late, for not doing great work, or for failing to overcome a challenge.

There is a moment between when something challenging happens to you and when you decide your response. That moment is where you get to decide what attitude you will choose; will you be the victim in your story or will you be the hero?

Heroes and victims have the same backstory: pain. The only difference is their response.

If the main character in a movie decides to view themselves as the victim, the story won't work because the story won't go anywhere. For a movie to go anywhere, the main character has to choose to play the hero. Heroes advance the story because heroes take action.

What do all successful people have in common? They see themselves as the hero in their life story rather than the victim.

Adversity is inevitable. Victimhood is optional. See yourself as the hero.

Chapter 2

It's Not Your

Turn

"Who we are when it's not our turn is more important than who we'll be when it is."

- Heather Thompson-Day

My senior year of college basketball was supposed to be my big year. I showed up to pre-season workouts in the best shape of my life. I had shed 15 pounds in the summer of 2020. I was trimmer and stronger than I had ever been, and my IQ was higher than it had ever been.

During the first week of school, I broke my hand. I had surgery a few weeks later that installed 5 small screws into my hand. I had complications throughout the season with the screws and ended the season with a second fracture in the same hand. I played 3 minutes the entire season.

This was my second season in a row with a season-ending injury, but this one ended my career. The whole season I showed up, clapped, and cheered when all I wanted to do was cry.

In the world of athletics, it's a race to the top of the ladder. Everyone wants to play 40 minutes a game. Everyone wants to lead their team in scoring. Everyone wants to be the best. We are constantly chasing perfection, success, wins, and awards. No one wants to be the benchwarmer. But there I was injured, at the end of the bench, knowing my career was over.

It's not like I was an underclassman with the hope that my time was coming. My time had come and gone. I was sentenced to the bench for the rest of my career.

So what do you do when it's not your turn? What do you do when someone else gets the starting position? The playing time you wanted? The promotion? The award you worked for? How do you encourage others when all you want to do is cry?

You show up and clap anyway. What if it's not about the destination, what we achieve, or how many minutes per game we average? What if it's about the journey? What if it's about who we become in the process?

Now I would be lying if I said that was my initial reaction to my injury. I can't even count the number of mental breakdowns I had in my hand surgeon's office. I was tired. I've had more than my share of injuries throughout my career, and I just wanted a healthy senior season of college basketball. I was burnt out from being injured. I was burnt out from physical therapy, doctor's appointments, watching practices, and riding the bench. I was at an all-time low. *And that's okay.*

When adversity hits, you don't have to pretend to be okay. It's okay not to be okay. Not being okay means you're holding the weight of your emotions rather than hiding from them; that's the strongest thing you can do. Grieving is the first step of healing. If you don't acknowledge the negative emotions, you can't move to the positive ones. The truth is that at first, adversity sucks. It gets better.

Role ≠ Value

The greatest lie ingrained into athletes is that you have to perform well in order to be loved. My biggest mistake was confusing my role with my value. I thought because I wasn't playing, I didn't matter. In reality, everyone is of equal and infinite value, regardless of what your role is. Just because you are a starter doesn't mean you are more important than anybody else. Just because you are a benchwarmer doesn't mean you are less important than anybody else. Your role is not your value.

There's a big misconception in sports that if we perform well, then we are loved and valued, and if we don't perform well, we aren't loved or valued. That couldn't be further from the truth. You are loved and valued regardless of whether or not you ever set foot on the court.

My role was to help the team by running the clock at practice and encouraging my teammates. It's definitely not the role I dreamed of when I imagined playing college basketball. But it was my role, and I had to own it.

I realized I had a choice that could shape my character for the rest of my life. I could view myself as the victim and I could sulk on the end of the bench, or I could clap when it wasn't my turn.

It's Not Your Turn

The year prior to my senior year, right before Covid hit, I had met with my public speaking professor, Heather Thompson-Day, who was writing a book called, *It's Not Your Turn: What To Do While You're Waiting For Your Breakthrough.* So throughout my senior year, I kept telling myself, "Julie, it's not your turn." Her book covers the question, "What do we do in the wait when it's not our turn?"

I came to this conclusion: at the end of your career, people will forget how many points you scored, they will forget how many minutes per game you averaged, and they will forget which accolades you won, but they will never forget what kind of teammate you were. That is what is most important. So I decided to play the one string I had left—my attitude. My only goal during my senior season was to be a great teammate.

That may seem like an easy thing to aspire to be, but it was far from easy. It was hard to get out of bed, let alone show up and cheer on my teammates. I fought back tears every game, every practice, and every film session. I so desperately wanted to be healthy and to be able to contribute on the court.

What do you do when the end of the bench is as good as it gets? You make yourself better during the wait.

As Heather put it in her book, "You can't control your circumstances, but you can control how you show up to them. What if some seasons are temporary, and we can make ourselves better in the waiting room?"

Redefining Success

In the world of sports, we define success in terms of results: starting, playing, scoring, and winning. As an injured player on the bench, none of those things were going to be possible for me. It couldn't be about the results, it had to be about the process. I had to redefine success as being a great teammate.

Sports culture acknowledges results first and character second. My mantra became, "Character first, results second." For me, there weren't going to be any results. All I had was my character. At the end of the day, that's all any of us have. All glory is fleeting, but character is what lasts. You can't always control results, but you are 100% in control of your character. In the wise words of my professor Heather Thompson-Day, "Who we are when it's not our turn is more important than who we'll be when it is."

The beauty of being sidelined is how it reveals your character. Who you are when you don't get the starting spot, don't get the promotion, or don't make the team is more important than who you will be when you do. John Wooden said it best, "Who you are as a person is more important than who you are as a player."

As a freshman in college, I averaged 40 minutes a game. As a sophomore in college, I averaged 20 minutes a game. As a junior, I averaged 3 minutes a game. As a senior, I played a total of 3 minutes. I was plagued with injuries and illnesses that ultimately ended my career early.

Brad Stevens went through something similar. As he put it, "I played a lot as a freshman, about the same as a sophomore, less as a junior, hardly at all as a senior. At the time, that was really hard to kind of grasp... This game is about how you act as a teammate. This game is about what you do from the standpoint of supporting one another, embracing roles, accepting roles... Those other things are a lot more important than how many minutes you play in a game, how many points you score."

I used to think this game was about what I could achieve, now I know it's more about who I become.

My senior year was painful, even more so mentally than physically, but I wouldn't trade it for the world because of what it taught me. I learned how to show up and clap for others when it's not my turn, and that who you are when you're benched is more important than who you are when you're on the court. Sometimes changing your perspective is more important than fixing the problem. You can't always fix the problem, but you can always fix your perspective.

Keep Showing Up

My advice is simple: keep showing up. Even when you want to cry, even when it feels like you're trudging through hell. It's easy to show up when you're a starter and there is a crowd screaming your name. The real test of your character is showing up to sit on the bench when there's no chance you'll get in the game.

Chances are if you're reading this book it's because you're up against some adversity. Perhaps it's not your turn right now. Maybe you're sick, injured, or discouraged. This too shall pass. But while you're going through it, you might as well learn, grow, and transform into a better version of yourself. It may not be your turn to be the star right now, but this season of life is still important. Because like Dr. Day said, "Who we are when it's not our turn is more important than who we'll be when it is." So show up and clap for others, even when it's not your turn.

Chapter 3

Logotherapy

"In some ways, suffering ceases to be suffering at the moment it finds a meaning."
- Dr. Viktor Frankl

What is our chief desire in life? Psychologists have debated the answer to this question for years.

Sigmund Freud believed our chief desire in life was pleasure. Alfred Adler believed our chief desire in life was power. Viktor Frankl contended that our chief desire was meaning, but when we can't find meaning in our lives, we try to distract ourselves with pleasure and power.

Think about the culture we live in. Numbing and distracting ourselves with pleasure is so ingrained in our culture that we don't even realize we are doing it. Our society has normalized getting addicted to everything from accomplishment and praise on social media to drugs and alcohol. Because there is an absence of meaning in our culture, we try to distract ourselves with pleasure, but it never satisfies.

People have not created meaning in their lives, so they're running around thinking the next promotion, the next car, or the next accomplishment will make them happy. As soon as they get the next thing, they realize that's empty too. They are in a constant, blind chase for meaning and fulfillment, but they don't even realize that's what they need. So they just keep chasing more things instead of creating a meaningful life.

Along with being a psychiatrist and neurologist, Viktor Frankl was a holocaust survivor. His pregnant wife, brother, mother, and father were all killed in Nazi concentration camps. To outsiders, it seemed as though he had lost everything. Frankl didn't believe that. As he put it, "Everything can be taken from a man but one thing: the last of human freedoms - to choose one's attitude in any given set of circumstances, to choose one's own way." In other words, no matter what happens to you, you can still choose your attitude and your response.

Frankl is the founder of logotherapy, which means "healing through meaning". The main idea behind logotherapy is that lack of meaning in our lives is the source of feelings of emptiness, stress, depression, boredom, and anxiety. Logotherapy was designed to help Viktor Frankl's patients to find meaning in their lives which would then reduce feelings of emptiness, stress, depression, boredom, and anxiety in their lives.

Everyone faces adversity. No one goes through life untested. What makes going through these hardships much more painful is the notion that this is not supposed to be happening. Viktor Frankl got his patients to find meaning in their struggles to make it more endurable. As he worded it, "In some ways, suffering ceases to be suffering at the moment it finds a meaning." Similarly, Friedrich Nietzsche said, "He who has a why to live can bear almost any how." When you know your pain has a purpose, it makes it worth it.

Dr. Frankl believed this universal drive for meaning and purpose in our life was conscious and subconscious. This means, if we have a deep dissatisfaction, we may not even be aware that the reason is because our life lacks meaning. We might have no idea why we are depressed and anxious. Oftentimes we attribute it to poor external circumstances, but it might actually be from a void of meaning.

Not only did Frankl believe lack of meaning was the source of a lot of problems in our lives, but he also believed that meaning is what motivates us. Meaning is what drives us, it gets us out of bed in the morning and fuels every action we take.

This matters because we have been given a significant amount of agency. If you feel like your life does not have meaning, you control the narrative. If you think life is meaningless, you can create a meaningful life. Dr. Frankl helped his patients create that meaning.

Have you lost your motivation? Do you feel empty, stressed, depressed, bored, or anxious? If you want motivation that lasts, you need to find more meaning in your life. *Purpose* is the key to psychological well-being.

Even within the concentration camps, Dr. Frankl found meaning by trying to help other prisoners with their psychological health by helping them fight off depression and trying to prevent suicides. Viktor Frankl was brought into the Viennese hospitals because the suicide rate was so high. He worked with over 30,000 suicidal patients. He never lost a patient.

There are a few aspects of logotherapy that Viktor Frankl believed would make someone's life meaningful:

1. If this were the second time you were about to live this day, how would you live it differently?

Every morning, pretend you have already made the mistakes that you might make, and don't make them. This is the act of learning from your mistakes before you make them. This approach forces us to live with intention. Take a look at your schedule today and see where you might be tempted to slack off, where you are likely to be low energy, and where you are likely to get distracted and correct those mistakes before they happen. In Frankl's words, "So live as if you were living already for the second time and as if you had acted the first time as wrongly as you are about to act now!"

2. Have a project that needs you.

Dr. Frankl believed creating something or accomplishing something would give our lives meaning. But it was more than just the event that would give life meaning, it was the process. He wanted his patients to wake up every day knowing that there was a project that needed them. This gave them the mindset that there was something that needed to get done and it wouldn't get done if they were to lay in bed all day. They had to have the mentality that they were *needed* and that bad things would happen if they didn't contribute to society and take action today.

3. Life offers you purpose and meaning; it does not owe you a sense of fulfillment or happiness.

The hardest working people and the most joyful people don't walk around thinking the world owes them something. The phrase, "I deserve" is not in their vocabulary. They see the opportunities and they believe they are responsible for earning what they want. Entitlement is a disempowering mindset. Responsibility is an empowering mindset. You don't deserve anything. You are responsible for doing what it takes to earn what you want.

4. Find a redemptive perspective of your adversity.

Viktor Frankl believed that no matter what had happened, you could find something good about it. After injuring his back in his very first college game, Michael Porter Jr. spent most of the season injured. After one year of college, Michael declared for the NBA draft. At one point during his high-school career, Michael Porter Jr. was projected to be picked first in the NBA draft. So when draft night came around, it was a shock to not hear his name called until the 14th pick.

For most, being drafted in the NBA is the most exciting night of their life, but all anyone could talk about was the "disappointment" of dropping to the 14th pick. In his interview, right after being drafted, he said, "All I can say is it's a blessing, you know I'm not entitled to this, everything's a blessing and I'm so excited. My path was a little different than everybody else's, but I'm going to make sure this pick is this organization's best pick they've ever made. I'm just happy to be with a team that believes in me. I don't feel entitled to this, it's a blessing."

He could have lost perspective and viewed the night as a disappointment and he would have lost one of the most exciting nights of his life. Most people saw the night as a huge disappointment for him, but how rare is it to get drafted in the NBA? Most people can only dream of making it that far, and rather than believing he deserved to get picked higher, Michael found the right perspective.

Finding the right perspective means you take a step back from the situation to evaluate what is most important; which is exactly what Michael Porter Jr. did here. When you are able to find the right perspective, you will lose the entitlement, and instead, you'll be full of gratitude, motivation, and joy.

Just by finding the perspective of gratitude, Michael turned what many saw as a disappointment into an exciting night of recognizing how blessed and grateful he was.

Chapter 4

Hero's Journey

"A hero is someone who has given his or her life to something bigger than oneself."
-    Joseph Campbell

We need stories. Stories are how our brains make sense of the world. Right before kids go to bed, typically their last request is to be told a bedtime story. We grow into adults with the same craving for stories, which is why movies are a billion-dollar industry. Even while we sleep, our brain is dreaming up stories.

Our brains are wired for stories. When we hear a story, our brain releases chemicals that make us feel pleasure, lower our stress levels, and make us more trusting. Stories are how we make sense of what is going on around us. Whenever there is a gap between what we know and what is happening, our brains will automatically make up a story to help us understand. Stories help us understand what is most important in life. Stories also help us feel in control. When we don't have a story to make sense of something, we feel out of control. When we lack stories, we lack meaning. Stories bring meaning, hope, control, and order to our lives.

Are you living a good story?

There's a good chance that you skimmed over that question without taking a moment to truthfully answer it. You probably read it, but it probably didn't impact you enough to make you ponder your life. So I will ask you again: Are you living a good story?

I'm not asking if something interesting has happened to you. I'm not asking if you can tell a good story or if you know a good story.

Are you *living* a good story?

If someone wanted to make a movie about your life, how much would they have to edit it to make it into an interesting and purposeful story worth watching? Is your life a page-turner, or would readers lose interest?

If people sat down in a movie theater to watch your life, would your life's story be worth eating popcorn to? Would the audience stay and linger as the credits rolled, thinking about the beauty of the story they had just watched? Would it give everyone watching a deeper sense of appreciation for their own life, or would they leave thinking, "What was that about?"

Most of our lives are too boring to remember. You will forget the vast majority of your life. We spend a lot of time sleeping, watching others' live good stories on TV, and doing things that are too boring to remember like brushing our teeth and washing the dishes. Think about the last year of your life; can you remember one event for each of the last 365 days?

Try to make a list of everything you remember from the past year. The list will likely just be a bunch of quick snapshots that aren't remembered in real-time. You're well aware you've had more experiences than the list shows, but you just don't remember.

If you look back on that list, there's a good chance it will seem like a bunch of random events. In the grand scheme of things, there's a good chance most of these memories will seem meaningless.

In movies, if a scene does not serve the plot, it gets deleted. If someone was making a movie about your life, how many scenes would they have to delete? How many hours, days, or even years of your life would belong in the deleted scenes?

If you watched a movie about a woman who wanted a Tesla you wouldn't cry at the end of the movie when she bought the Tesla. You wouldn't tell your friends about it unless it was warning them against seeing the movie. You would feel like you had wasted 2 hours and the movie probably wouldn't have any impact on your life. You would probably forget about the movie within a few days. The movie is too meaningless to remember. Selfish stories aren't memorable.

But we spend so much of our lives living those stories and wonder why we feel so unfulfilled. The same elements that make stories meaningful, make lives meaningful.

Are you living a good story? Does each day of your life serve the plot of your life or is it just a bunch of random events that belong in the deleted scenes?

So what makes a story meaningful?
- The character has to change (be flawed at the beginning)

47

- The character has to be good and want something good
- The character has to face resistance
- The character has to have doubt
- The character has to have a wise friend
- The character has to take action

Change

At the beginning of every story, the main character is flawed. If not, there is no story because the main character has to change. The entire story lies in the character arc.

In the same way, we are designed to change; mentally and physically. You were not designed to stay the same, you were meant to grow.

Every seven years, essentially you become a new person physically because every cell in your body has been replaced by a new one. If you want to lose weight or gain muscle, you can adjust the way you eat and exercise and you can change your physique. Similarly, your brain has a significant amount of plasticity; you can change the structure of it.

Your brain physically stops growing as a young adult, but it continues to change throughout your entire life. Neuroplasticity refers to our brain's ability to adapt and change. This means our brains are constantly forming and rewiring neural connections. This means those hardwired things about you can actually change.

Think about something you hate doing; maybe it's running sprints, eating vegetables, or doing laundry. If you write a 1-page paper about why you actually *love* that thing, you will rewire the neural pathways in your brain, and you will psychologically begin to like that thing that you hate.

At the beginning of all great stories, the main character is pretty flawed. By the end of the story, the character has changed. The hero goes from being a jerk in the beginning to being kind and empathetic at the end. The hero goes from being afraid in the beginning to being brave at the end. The character has to change if the story is going to be any good.

If you want to live a good story, you have to change. You should constantly be in the process of becoming a better version of yourself. To live a good story, never stop growing and changing. If the point of the story is character transformation, that is also what will make your life more meaningful.

Want Something Good

In Blake Snyder's book called *Save The Cat: The Last Book on Screenwriting You'll Ever Need*, he reveals a trick in screenwriting called "saving the cat". Whether you are aware of it or not, most movies begin by having the main character do charity.

In The Incredibles, Mr. Incredible starts the movie by literally saving a cat while simultaneously stopping a high-speed, armed police chase.

In The Hunger Games, the first time we see Katniss, she is comforting her little sister who is screaming from a nightmare. Katniss then sings her back to sleep.

The beginning of Rudy consists of almost everyone telling him that he is too small to play football at Notre Dame and that he's not smart enough to go there. It would have been easy for Rudy to disrespectfully push back, but he doesn't, and you can tell he is a good guy.

Why? It makes us trust the character and root for them. If movies started with the main character bullying people around, we wouldn't want them to win, so we would have no reason to keep watching. The beginning of every good story is supposed to make you care about the characters so you will stay interested in the story.

If you want to live a good story, you have to be clear about what you want. If you're watching a movie and halfway through, you still have no idea what the main character wants, you'll probably lose interest. We knew within the first three minutes of Rudy that he wanted to play college football at Notre Dame.

If the ambition of the character is selfish, the story normally won't work. If their ambition is to help feed hungry children, everyone wants them to win.

For example, Rocky wanted to be the heavyweight champion of the world. This is a pretty selfish ambition, but it worked because Rocky spends the first hour of every movie saving the cat, and we always want the good guy to win.

Get clear on what you want. Make sure your intentions are pure. If the reason why you want what you want is good, it will be worth it.

Face Resistance

The average person is exposed to about 9,000 ads each day. The ads all follow a similar formula: convince you that you aren't happy or satisfied, and your life will be better and you will be more fulfilled if you buy the product or service. This means you are being told 9,000 times each day that you are not happy. This also means we as a society, seek comfort and avoid pain. So when we do face resistance, we have this idea that it's not *supposed* to happen, that we are not *supposed* to feel pain or deal with conflict. This idea that we are always supposed to feel comfortable is a lie.

If you watched a movie and the main character never faced resistance, it would be a really boring movie, and you wouldn't remember it. The hero *has* to face resistance for the story to be any good. The greater the conflict, the longer the journey, and the more adversity, *the better the story will be.*

Nobody remembers easy stories.

- Walt Disney was told he was not creative enough and had no good ideas.
- Oprah Winfrey was told she was not cut out for television and was fired for getting too emotionally invested in her stories.
- Einstein did not speak until he was four years old.
- Michael Jordan and Bob Cousy were both cut from their high school basketball team.
- Bill Walsh didn't win a single game in his first season as an NFL Head Coach.
- Beethoven was told he was hopeless as a composer.
- Benjamin Franklin dropped out of school at the age of 10.
- Professional surfer Bethany Hamilton had her arm bitten off by a shark.
- Thomas Edison had around 10,000 failed attempts when trying to invent the light bulb.

Adversity brings something out of us that ease never could. It ignites a greater passion in us. We don't know what we're really made of until we face adversity. Adversity reveals our character. We don't become the best version of ourselves when everything is easy. We grow into the best version of ourselves during the toughest times. Oftentimes our passion is realized during the toughest times of our lives. That's when we find our purpose. Obstacles are put in our path to see how bad we really want something. If what you want is trivial, like fame or money, those dreams normally die out at the first sign of difficulty. However, if what you want is tied to a great and meaningful purpose, you will be willing to persist when others have given up.

"Without the rain there is no beauty in the summer. Rain gives depth, it gives roots. If a plant is only exposed to sun and no rain, it becomes dry, flimsy, and dead. Too many times we curse the rain in our lives—suffering, trials, hardships—

but the truth is without rain nothing grows."

- Jefferson Bethke

We recognize that great stories require adversity, until the adversity happens to us, then we think it's unfair. What if whenever we face resistance, instead of immediately asking, "Why me?" and thinking about how unfair it is, we start thinking about the great story we are living in?

Think of adversity as an inciting incident. The inciting incident is what really starts a story; it's the dramatic event that sets the story in motion and forces the character to change. When screenwriters are attempting to come up with the inciting incident, oftentimes they will ask, "What is the worst thing that could happen to the main character?" Then they will write that into the screenplay. This is counterintuitive to how we act. We avoid the worst things that could happen to us, but good stories embrace it. The main character does not choose to change, an event forces them to change.

Without an inciting incident, the story doesn't go anywhere. If the character does not have any problems, there is no story. If Katniss does not volunteer as tribute in The Hunger Games, the story doesn't happen. Yet we have been told to avoid adversity. As Levi Lusko put it, "Comfort zones don't keep our lives safe, they keep our lives small." You were not put on this earth to live a small life. You were not put here to hide out in your comfort zone and get as comfortable as possible. You are here for a greater purpose, and to live out that purpose, you are going to have to get out of your comfort zone and face resistance.

If you want to live a good and meaningful story, you are going to have to face resistance with courage. The story won't be any good if you merely try to "get through" the adversity. Heroes don't hide out and wait for the conflict to go away, they have to face it head-on. The hero in every story uses adversity as a catalyst to help them become a better version of themselves. Whatever horrible things have happened to them, they *own* it, and they embrace that part of their story. As Brene Brown puts it, "When we own our story, we can write a brave new ending."

Adversity is embedded into your story for a purpose. Setbacks, obstacles, discomfort, losses, pain, failures, and tough times are embedded into your story for a reason. You can't live a good story without facing resistance. Embrace it. Leaders are not made in smooth seas when everything is going well. It's easy to lead when you are winning. Leaders are made in the storm. No one is born tough. Toughness is built in the struggle.

Adversity is the best teacher, and the lessons are maturity, strength, wisdom, toughness, resilience, empathy, perspective, determination, patience, and courage. Embrace adversity, you will develop your character.

Have Doubt

Before the character moves into the next act, they are filled with doubt. They are unsure of whether or not they can do it. They debate whether or not they should take action. The hero always second-guesses himself. He starts to realize that what he's about to do is crazy. The hero realizes how daunting the task ahead is. He thinks about how unqualified he is for the endeavor. It occurs to the hero that he might not have what it takes. At this point of the story, all the character can think about is how dangerous, risky, and difficult what he needs to do is. Ultimately, the character decides he has no other choice because he cannot stay where he is.

When a lot of us experience doubt, we decide we are unqualified. We figure that if we were meant to be one of the greats, we would not have any doubt. That is a false narrative. Doubt is part of the hero's journey. If you aren't full of doubt, you need a bigger ambition. Doubt qualifies you. If you feel unsure of whether or not you are capable, it's a good sign you're on the right path.

Have a Wise Friend

When the character is full of doubt, the wise friend comes along and guides the hero into taking action. This is the Yoda, or mentor, or guide of the story. One of the main differences between the wise friend and the hero is that while the hero has to change, the wise friend doesn't change. The wise friend has already been there and done that. The wise friend not only offers their presence to the main character, but they also offer a plan. No one pursuing greatness is going to be able to do it alone. We need wise friends. Seek out wise friends.

Take Action

This is the most difficult part of the hero's journey.

The hero has to take action. If the hero does not take action, there is no story. The hero has to do stuff.

The stories we tell ourselves are very different from the stories we are telling the world. Why? Because all the world sees is what you do. You might think you are the most passionate basketball player on the planet, but if you never take action on that, you are the same as every other basketball player. There is a dissonance between who we think we are and who the world knows us to be. We get an idea and we keep it to ourselves as brain candy instead of acting on it. We spend a lot more time *thinking* rather than *doing*. The world does not know our thoughts or feelings, the world only knows us by our actions. A character is what he does, not what he thinks about or feels. It's what we *do* that counts. You can't daydream your way into living a great story. You have to make moves to live a meaningful life.

You have been given a significant amount of agency over your life. You don't have to sit back and wait for life to happen to you. You can actually grab the pen and write your own story, but you have to take action.

"Character cannot be developed in ease and quiet. Only through experience of trial and suffering can the soul be strengthened, vision cleared, ambition inspired and success achieved."
- Helen Keller

Chapter 5

The Power of Words

"The power of life and death are in the tongue, and we eat the fruit of them. We cannot have a negative mouth and a positive life."
-    Joyce Meyer

Research has found that about 80% of our thoughts are negative. Thoughts become words, and the average person says around 16,000 words every day. That's 12,800 negative words we are saying each day if we don't flip the script.

Most of us simply say whatever comes to mind without giving it a second thought. Here's the problem with that: we are so prone to negativity.

Because of our brain's negative bias, if we get 1 piece of criticism and 4 compliments, our brain perceives that as neutral. If you want to even be considered a slightly positive person, you need a 5 to 1 ratio of compliments to criticisms.

Here's an easy way to tell if someone needs encouragement: *if they are breathing.* Everyone needs encouragement and they need a lot more of it than you think, no one is exempt.

What can hold us back from living a good story? Words.
What can launch us into living a good story? Words.

Words can help or hurt us.

Words can build us up or tear us down.

Words can shape or scar us.

Words can fill us with hope or limit us.

Get really picky with your words.

Once you realize how powerful your thoughts and words are, you become more selective about which ones you use. The right words at the right time can change everything, and we can be the ones to say them.

There is one person you listen to more than anyone else: *you.* Words matter, especially the ones you say to yourself. Henry Ford said it best, "Whether you think you can or whether you think you can't, you're right."

Thoughts become words.

Words become actions.

Actions become habits.

Habits become your character.

What's the story you're telling yourself?

If you're not telling yourself a good story about

who you are and where your life is going, you aren't going to be able to live a good story.

Words become self-fulfilling prophecies. Words reveal our expectations, and our lives follow our expectations. When we *expect* something to happen, we behave in a way that makes it much more likely to happen.

Expect to win.

Expect to perform well.

Expect to have a good day.

Expect greatness from those around you.

Make great expectations a habit. Living a meaningful life requires you to believe great narratives about yourself.

You are a leader.

You are a genius.

You are a difference-maker.

Leaders, geniuses, and difference-makers are not born, they're made. All you have to do is choose to believe you are one. You can believe these things are true or false, but if you believe they are true, your life will get better and a lot more interesting. If you refuse to believe these things, you can't live a good story. If you don't believe these things, you might miss your purpose. If you are a leader, a genius, and a difference-maker, you have a lot more responsibilities; you have to solve problems, care for and help people.

Believing these things about yourself comes with a determined optimism because you now have to show up and give your best. These beliefs will change your character and make you more resilient because they are about your identity.

There is a big difference between telling someone they did a good job leading and telling someone they are a great leader. There's a big difference between telling someone they made a good play and telling someone they are a play-maker.

The most powerful kind of encouragement is identity-based.

When someone makes a mistake, the most powerful thing you can say to them is, "That's not who you are." What you do is driven by who you think you are. Tell people who you want them to become, including yourself.

In fact, you should lie to people. Lie in an empowering way that brings out the potential for greatness inside of people. Sometimes greatness is buried below insecurity and fear, it's a leader's job to call it out. Here is why: calling out the greatness you see in people, *brings* out greatness in people.

In her Ted Talk titled "The Opportunity of Adversity," Aimee Mullins references a case study done in a school in Britain in the 1960's. Over a 3 month period, they took all of the D-level students and gave them A's. By the end of the 3 months, those students were performing at an A-level. At the beginning of the 3 months, the A-level students were also given D's. By the end of the 3 months, they were performing at a D-level. The teachers had no idea the switch was made, so they had been telling the D-students how bright, smart, and brilliant they were, and they became it.

People will rise or fall to the level of whoever you tell them they are. More importantly, *you* will rise or fall to the level of whoever *you* tell yourself you are. Why? Words instill in us hope that we can change. And if we need to change in order to live a good story and a more meaningful life, we need to use words that help us to change for the better.

If you tell someone every day that they are a leader, they will become one, even if it isn't true at first. If you tell someone they're a difference-maker, they will make a difference. If you tell someone they are a genius, they will become one. It's okay to prematurely call out the potential for greatness you see in people. Our words have power because we believe our words, other people do too.

If you tell yourself you aren't creative, you probably won't come up with anything creative.

If you tell yourself you aren't a good communicator, you'll find yourself in a lot of miscommunications.

Stop telling yourself dumb narratives.

When we expect something to happen, we behave in a way that makes it more likely to happen. We live into whatever narratives we tell ourselves.

If you tell yourself that you are a winner, you will play in a way that makes you a lot more likely to win.

If you tell yourself you are creative, don't be surprised when you create ideas no one else has thought of.

Tell yourself positive narratives that are true or even that you wish were true. You will act in a way that turns them into a reality. Words have power. Don't just listen to yourself, *talk* to yourself.

The Ticket

In March 2018, Virginia's men's basketball program lost to UMBC in the first round of the NCAA tournament. Virginia was the overall #1 seed while UMBC was a #16 seed. It was the most improbable upset in the history of the men's college basketball tournament.

At the beginning of the next season, Tony Bennett showed his team a Tedx Talk called, "How The Story Transforms The Teller" by Donald Davis. As a five-year-old boy, Donald's father, Joe had accidentally taken an ax to his knee and become crippled. After his surgery, his mother told him it was time to tell the story. He told his mom he didn't want to tell the story because it wouldn't change the fact that he was crippled. His mother replied, "You're not telling the story to change what happened. You're telling the story to change you." His mother made him tell the story over and over again.

She would make him tell the story with the focus on what he learned by living through it.

She would make him tell the story with the focus on what others around him learned.

She would make him tell the story with the focus on what he *gets to* do now that he's crippled that others don't get to do.

By the time he was 15 years old, he had told the story so many times with a redemptive perspective that he decided chopping his leg was the best thing he had ever done in his life. Joe attributed his success as a banker to being crippled. Joe said, "It is never, never tragic when something people think is bad happens to you. Because, if you could learn to use it right, it could buy you a ticket to a place you would never have gone any other way."

> *"Show me someone who has done something worthwhile, and I'll show you someone who has overcome adversity."*
>
> - *Lou Holtz*

In a storybook comeback, Virginia won the National Championship the year after being on the wrong side of the most improbable upset. After the win in the post-game press conference, Virginia Head Coach Tony Bennett said:

"I'll mention what happened last year: that can only mature you. I don't know of anything else that would allow these guys to be able to handle this situation and to play through stuff, to have perspective, poise, and resilience unless they went through something that hard.

It makes for a great story. When we lost, we said we're not going to sweep it under the rug. We're gonna look at it. We're gonna grow from it. We're gonna face it head-on. We're not gonna obsess over it.

Yes, losing can produce some of the strongest, most painful emotions. But those emotions can be extremely useful, if you learn to harness them effectively. They can help you find motivation, focus, and most of all balance.

You talk about it being almost prophetic, what that quote says, 'If you learn to use it right, the adversity, it will buy you a ticket to a place you couldn't have gone any other way.' Going through what we did last year I think bought us a ticket to a national championship. At the time, you wouldn't have thought it, but they were battle-tested."

Virginia's point guard, Kyle Guy, agreed with his coach that the previous year's loss had prepared them. He stated: "I think we've taken every experience that we've been through together and used it in a way that could propel us to a National Championship."

Many people assumed the previous year's loss would continue to embarrass and haunt Virginia, but that was not the mentality they had. Tony Bennett described last year's loss as a "painful *gift*." Coach Bennett explained that the loss had sparked a fire in him. There is no doubt that fire was in everyone on the team, as they came back the next year determined to write a better ending to the story, with extra motivation from the heartbreaking loss.

Imagine if Coach Bennett wouldn't have described the loss as a gift. Imagine if instead of describing the loss as, "buying them a ticket to a place they could not have gone any other way," he would have swept it under the rug or complained about it. Where others saw a problem, Coach Bennett saw an opportunity. That's what great leaders do. It's one thing to "get through" the adversity, but Coach Bennett's mentality went beyond that. Virginia *embraced* the adversity, they owned the narrative. They lived a good story and they wrote the storybook ending.

We can't avoid the adversity in our lives, but we can reframe it. We can decide the context of the adversity. We get to decide what the adversity means to us. We decide the role that it will play in our story. If we hide from the difficult parts of our lives, we give up our control of the narrative. If we tell the story, we have power over the adversity. Setbacks are inevitable, but setbacks don't define you. What you do next does. What counts are the words you use to frame the adversity and how you respond to it.

Chapter 6

Success
Changes
Nothing

"When I meet with the players,
what strikes me is that they are
truly unhappy."
-    Adam Silver

Have you ever lost passion for something you love?

When we shift our focus from things that are not the point, we lose our passion.

After winning his second National Championship as the Head Men's basketball coach at the University of Florida, Billy Donovan was depressed. In his words:

"I was depressed. I lost total sight of what it's all about, and I don't mean what it's all about in terms of what goes into winning, but the fact that it doesn't change your life one bit, other than someone may write next to your name, 'national champion coach.' Outside of that, it does not change your life. The first time it really resonated with me was I saw an interview on *60 Minutes* with Tom Brady when I think the Patriots had won three of their five Super Bowls and after the third one he asked himself, 'Is this what it's all about?' he added, 'Because at the end of the day if it's all about the ring and the trophy, you lose the most valuable thing, and it's the group of people working together to accomplish something they couldn't accomplish on their own.'"

Billy Donovan was depressed because he lost sight of what it was all about for him as a coach: the people. Because he made it about winning, he lost his passion.

NBA players are rich, famous, successful, and unhappy.

The total NBA revenue in the 2021-2022 season was around 10 billion dollars. The NBA is more visible than it's ever been. Every game is live-streamed. NBA players are celebrities. Every move they make, outfit they wear, song they listen to, and place they go is admired by fans. NBA players are superstars. They are paid more money than most people could ever dream of. They've made it to the highest level of basketball. They have the accolades, the fans, the success, the fame, the money; they are living the life most people dream of, so you would think they'd all be happy, but they're not.

In an interview at the Sports Analytics Conference, NBA Commissioner Adam Silver said,

"I think we live in the age of anxiety. When I meet with the players, what strikes me is that they are truly unhappy. This is not some show they're putting on for the media. When I'm one-on-one with a lot of these guys, I think to the outside world, they see the fame, the money, all the trappings that go with it, they're the best in the world at what they do, they say *how is it possible they could even be complaining?* A lot of these young men are genuinely unhappy. Some of them are amazingly isolated. This goes back to Jordan, in Michael's last season with the bulls, I mean the camaraderie was incredible. There was classic team-building going on all the time, these guys were a band of brothers; on the buses on the planes, and all the attention only brought them closer. If you're around a team in this day and age, their headphones are on, they're isolated and their head is down. I remember years ago, Isiah Thomas said to me, "Championships are won on the bus." and he meant that. The reality is most don't want to play together. There's enormous jealousy amongst our players, everybody's got to be the alpha. The best teams have relationships and maybe this is why the Bulls and the Spurs were so high-functioning. I had a conversation with a superstar player, he was playing a game Friday night and their next game was Sunday night in Miami. He said to me, from the time I get on the plane to the time I show up in the arena on Sunday, I won't see a single person. And he said to me, 'I know if I said this publicly, people would say poor baby.' He was incredibly lonely, but to the point where it was almost a pathology, it wasn't just hey I'm lonely, it was a deep sadness. They're real issues."

Adam Silver began this conversation by talking about the players constantly shifting teams in the NBA; implying that there is an underlying belief in some players that *if* I can be on this team and *if* we can win *then* I'll be happy, but that's never the case. External achievement or circumstances can't fulfill us internally. Winning is fleeting. It changes nothing about who you are as a person because a win is just an event.

Our society has been fed the lie that success will lead to happiness. We believe once we reach a certain level of achievement, a certain number in our bank account, a certain level of ease, or a certain number of followers, we will be happy. We think *if* everything goes right and the difficulties go away, then we will be happy.

Yet, there are people who have millions of fans, make hundreds of millions of dollars playing a game, and they are still not happy. Clearly, this logic that success will bring us happiness and fulfillment is flawed, but we still expect it. So many people win or make it to the next level and their first thought is *that's it?*

If success bred happiness, NBA players would be some of the most fulfilled people on the planet, but they aren't. Success does not breed happiness, because external achievement can't change you internally.

A successful season, an award, a trophy, or a banner can't turn you into a happy person; it will feel good for a little while, then you'll need something else or something more. There's always the next game or the next season. We're always being compared to something or someone better, especially because of social media.

This doesn't mean winning and success aren't worthy pursuits. You should always play to win. However, there are things even more worthy of pursuing that will bring us lasting motivation and fulfillment, no matter what our circumstances are: excellence, relationships, and joy. What really matters is the pursuit of excellence, building relationships, and choosing joy.

Joy vs. Happiness

The root word of happiness is hap, meaning chance or luck. We see 'hap' in words like perhaps and happen because happiness is an emotional response to an event that occurred. Happiness is purely circumstantial, it can only occur under certain conditions.

For example, happiness comes with statements like: If I win, I will be happy or if I score this many points I'll be happy. If I can be healthy, then I'll be happy. If things go my way, then I'll be happy. And when we achieve these things, we feel good for a little while, but then it wears off and we need something else for us to be happy. Of course, no one wins every game, no one averages 50 points per game, and no one goes through life without encountering adversity, so relying on happiness will leave you unsatisfied a lot.

Joy is much different. Joy is not a response to a result. Joy is a choice. Joy is the attitude we have when we're doing something we believe in, something that gives us purpose, or something we love, regardless of the results. We see joy in words like enjoy and rejoice. Joy has nothing to do with results or circumstances, it's purely inward.

When you choose joy, the work is the reward, the result is irrelevant.

Wanting to win a game and do well are worthy aspirations, but what happens in the offseason, when there are no games, or if you're injured and can't play? If you rely on happiness, the offseason will be miserable and injuries will be unbearable. You will enjoy your life, basketball, and the process of becoming a great player a lot more when you let go of the need for a certain outcome, and focus on the belief that you're doing something you're *meant* to do, something you *love* to do, and something you *get* to do.

Joy is based on your outlook, not on something that happens to you. You can't always control your circumstances, but you can always control your outlook. Joy can be present during unhappy or happy times. It is a constant perspective of seeing the enjoyment in what you are *doing*, not what you are getting. Happiness is tied to an event, joy is simply tied to your attitude.

Cheerfulness In The Face Of Adversity

It's pretty easy to smile after a win. We smile when we're comfortable and having a good time. It's counterintuitive to smile while experiencing difficulties, but that's when you need it most.

Cheerfulness in the face of adversity is one of the Royal Marines' mottos. It sounds optimistic, but studies are now proving that it actually increases our endurance. When most people face adversity, they often find themselves completely exhausted, even if they aren't exerting themselves physically. Why? We get emotionally overwhelmed just by thinking about difficulties. It can be tempting to give up in the face of adversity, but if you want to come out of it stronger, face it with a smile.

Our brains are constantly taking inventory of our facial expressions. When we smile, our brain assumes we must be in a good mood, so our brains release positive chemicals that make us feel uplifted.

Stronger With a Smile

There is a constant facial feedback loop going on. Not only do we smile because we're in a good mood, but we can also create a good mood just by smiling. There was a study done recently where athletes cycled until they were completely exhausted. As they cycled, they were either shown pictures of people smiling or frowning. However, they showed them the pictures so fast that it barely registered on a conscious level, it was completely subconscious.

Those who were subconsciously exposed to smiles were able to cycle for longer. Smiling literally enhances performance. If you are facing adversity, you have a long and tough battle ahead and you need endurance. You might not feel like smiling, but you can make the choice to do so anyway because you are stronger when you're smiling.

By no coincidence, Warriors Head Coach Steve Kerr prides himself on his team's most important core value: joy. "We basically covered the walls of our practice facility with pictures of our guys in action *smiling,* celebrating championships, holding up trophies; we wanted that joy to be visible on the walls of our facility." But more importantly, Steve Kerr and Steph Curry lead by example. Their joy is evident. They enjoy the game, they enjoy practice, and you can see it on their faces.

In the wise words of Pat Riley, "Great effort springs naturally from a great attitude." If you're going to make adversity your ally, you are going to need great effort, and it starts with a great attitude. Choose joy.

Here's where most people go wrong: they believe success will make their life more meaningful so they chase the wrong things. Success is an empty promise because it won't make your life more meaningful. In good stories, it's not even necessary for the main character to win, he just has to have a worthy pursuit, sacrifice, and give his absolute best for the cause. Success changes nothing because it does not magically bring meaning into your life. All glory is fleeting. Living a good story is more important than being successful by society's standards, because stories are meaningful and stories last. Your character is more important than your success.

Chapter 7

Committed To The Future

"If what you did yesterday still looks big to you, you haven't done much today."
- Mike Krzyzewski

Here's what's going to happen: you're going to read this book and get super motivated because living a good story and a meaningful life sounds like a good idea. You are going to want something good and want to take action. Then, you are going to realize that it's a lot harder than you thought it would be. You are going to be tempted to go looking for an easier story. You are going to want to look for a story that does not require as much out of you.

Don't. Don't you dare go looking for an easier story. No one ever promised that it would be easy, but it will be worth it. Understand that living a good story is hard. Becoming the best version of yourself is hard. Winning is hard. It's never easy, but it's always worth it.

If you want the strength, endurance, and the focus you need to be able to live a meaningful story, you need to commit to the future.

What are you more committed to: the future or the past? What are you more committed to: what's ahead of you, or what's behind you? What are you more committed to:

yesterday or today? Life moves in one direction and basketball moves in one direction: forward.

It's important to learn from the past and appreciate the past, but you can't live in the past.

Kobe Bryant was one of the greatest basketball players of all time. When he retired in 2016, he had a choice:

A.) He could be committed to the past. He could've been complacent. He could've relished in his illustrious career, sat around, and reminisced on the glory days. He made enough money to where he could have lived comfortably on vacation.

OR

B.) He could be committed to the future. He could use the lessons he learned in his basketball career to create a better future by sharing them with everyone else. He could keep moving forward, keep working, and keep believing the best is yet to come.

Kobe chose to be more committed to the future than the past.

Kobe was unlike most of the other great, retired professional athletes. Kobe didn't want to talk about his playing career. Kobe only wanted to talk about what was next. He found his next passion and put his otherworldly work ethic to use in his new endeavors. He started a training academy, wrote a few books, and he even won an Oscar, a feat some work their whole lives for and never achieve.

This wasn't a first for Kobe. Being committed to the future is the story of his career. Most basketball players, especially shooters, go through periods of time when they are not playing well or their shot is off. Most people refer to this as a slump or a funk. Kobe didn't believe in slumps. WNBA star Jewell Loyd once asked Kobe how to get out of a funk. Kobe replied, "No such thing as a funk. There's just the next shot." Kobe never focused on the past. He focused on what was next. No matter how many championships he won, how many injuries he had, or how many airballs he shot, he always showed up the next day, ready to work harder, rise earlier, and stay later than anyone else. Nothing could deter him from taking the next step toward the future he wanted.

Rosy Retrospect

Our human tendency is to stay committed to the past, especially when the present is challenging. There is a phenomenon known by psychologists as "rosy retrospection" which refers to our tendency to disproportionately remember the good times. It's counterintuitive to fully commit to what's ahead of you because it's so tempting to relish in the past. This is why leveling up is so hard, we get stuck in the past. Instead of being eager to improve, a lot of highly ranked high school players come into college their freshman year, and they spend all their time thinking about how great they were in high school. They think they can coast because of what they achieved in the past.

If you are not intentional about getting better and moving forward, you will find yourself coasting, and coasting never moves you uphill. If you are coasting, you are moving downhill.

Being committed to what's ahead of you means you have an attitude that is always looking forward, believing your best days are ahead, and a work ethic that is aligned with that belief.

The one constant in basketball and in life is change. It's a game of constant adjustments, and if you are not committed to the future, quick adjustments, constant growth, and change, you're going to lose. The game keeps going and life keeps going. Don't get stuck in the past.

How do you know where your commitment lies?

Your attitude:

Are you a know-it-all or a learn-it-all? Know-it-alls are done learning. They're committed to the past and to what they already know. Learn-it-alls are committed to the future. No matter how much they know or how much they've accomplished, they want more. Know-it-alls never get better. Learn-it-alls always get better.

Do you know what Michael Jordan said his best skill was? He said his best skill was that he was coachable. He described himself as a sponge and said he was aggressive to learn. By no coincidence, he is considered one of the greatest basketball players of all time. People who are committed to the future are not concerned with looking like an expert. All they care about is getting better, so they are always trying to learn.

The words, "We've always done it this way," are not in the vocabulary of those who are committed to the future. They keep being a student of the game, changing their mind, and finding new ways to do things that will better their future.

Maintain the attitude of a student, not an expert.

Your reaction:

When you're thinking about the next play, it shows in your body language. You're not sulking or whining about the last play. Instead of reacting negatively, you're engaged in the present. By focusing on the next play, you're ahead of the game. The game of basketball does not stop and wait for you to get over something. The game keeps going, and if you're complaining about the last play, you are behind. The game will move on with or without you.

The same is true in life. When you are more committed to the past than the future, you spend all of your time and energy focused on things you can't control. People who are committed to what is behind them waste their time complaining. It's okay to get sad but don't get stuck. People who are committed to the future don't waste time thinking about what they can't control. They have a quick recovery time. When something goes wrong, people who are committed to the future simply focus on taking the next step to the very best of their ability.

On December 10, 1914, there was a massive explosion in West Orange, New Jersey. Ten buildings in inventor Thomas Edison's plant were engulfed in flames. Multiple fire departments rushed to the scene, but the fire was too powerful to be put out quickly.

Charles Edison, Thomas Edison's son, recounts his dad saying as he watched the buildings burn, "It's all right. We've just got rid of a lot of rubbish. I'll start all over again tomorrow." Thomas Edison was 67 years old at the time. He could have cried, complained, or yelled in anger, but he accepted that there was nothing he could do to change it so he channeled all of his energy into a productive response. The next morning, he began rebuilding.

> *"The measure of who we are is how we react when something doesn't go our way."*
> - *Gregg Popovich*

Adversity doesn't define you, what you do next does. Will you waste all your energy sulking, or will you begin rebuilding?

Your work ethic:

When you're committed to the future, no amount of setbacks can keep you from working towards a better future, and no amount of success can either. Those who are committed to the future work hard to keep making progress, changing, learning, and growing. People who are committed to the future handle success the same way they handle failure: more work.

Your perspective:

When you are committed to the future you have an opportunistic mindset. You don't see positives or negatives, you see opportunities for development. People who are more committed to the future than the past are not optimists or pessimists, they are opportunists.

For example, when you're going through practice and a mistake is made, the coach normally says the word "baseline"; as in it's time to run sprints. Those who are committed to the past believe this to be *punishment*. Those who are committed to the future only view it as *training*. *Punishment* looks backward at the mistake, making you feel frustrated, leading to an unmotivated, half-hearted sprint. *Training* learns from the mistake and quickly looks forward to what this sprint is preparing you for. *Training* makes you feel motivated and excited about the future because you know it's going to better you, which leads to purposeful work. *Punishment* asks, "What did I do wrong?" *Training* asks, "What can I learn from what I did wrong?" *Punishment* keeps you stuck in the past because you get bitter wishing the past was different. *Training* helps you make progress because you are thinking about how much the discomfort you are going through *now* is going to prepare you for the future. Whatever "trouble" you are in is not punishment, it is training. Life is all a matter of perspective. Every obstacle you are currently facing is *preparing* you for who you were meant to become.

Commit to the future. Believe the best is ahead of you, and work to make it true.

Live in Hope

Michael Jordan once said, "Most people live in fear because they project the past into the future."

Are you living in hope or are you living in fear?

The Bible says, "Be not afraid," 365 times; one for every day of the year. This means *you are going to be afraid*; it's inevitable. This also means you shouldn't let fear control you. Fear is a manipulative emotion; it can keep you from using your gifts and trick you into living a boring life with a lack of purpose.

Fear tells us to stay in our comfort zone. The problem is, comfort zones don't keep us safe, they keep us in a small box where we are too scared to use our gifts and talents to help others. You can't lead from your comfort zone. As the University of Houston research professor and bestselling author Dr. Brené Brown puts it, "We have to be able to choose courage over comfort, we have to be able to say, 'Look I don't know if I'm going to nail this but I'm going to try.'"

Fear is inevitable, but courage is a choice. Courageous people experience the same fear as everyone else, they just don't let it stop them from taking action. Here's the problem with fear: it will keep you from trying. Here's the good thing about hope: it gives you a reason not to listen to fear.

We have a habit of spending a lot of time thinking about what could go wrong; what will happen if we lose, if disaster strikes, if our plans don't work, or if we miss a shot. The simple science is, whatever you're thinking about the most, is most likely to occur. If you get the opportunity to shoot the game-winner and you're thinking about what will happen if you miss, you're a lot more likely to miss.

If you want to perform at your best, fear can't be the most prominent thought. If you want to live a meaningful life, fear can't be the most prominent thought. Your actions subconsciously follow your thoughts. Think about swishing the shot, think about winning, and think about succeeding.

If you have dreams of being a great basketball player, you can't focus on fear. The more you think about fear, the more power you give fear in your life. The good news is your hopes and dreams work the same way. When you focus on your dreams, on what could go right, and on hope, you give your dreams more power than your fears. Roy Williams said it best, "We never need to be pushed by our problems, but led by our dreams." People who focus on fear are committed to the past. Have tunnel vision on your dreams, and stay committed to the future. Keep believing the best is yet to come and keep moving forward.

Chapter 8

The Dip

"Scarcity is the secret to value. If there wasn't a Dip, there would be no scarcity. Extraordinary benefits accrue to the tiny minority of people who are able to push just a tiny bit longer than most."
- Seth Godin

Seth Godin, author of *The Dip,* defines the dip as the long slow slog between starter and mastery. In his book, Seth talks about how there are only 2 ways through the dip:

- Quit. You can quit and waste everything you've invested, without ever seeing the results you were working towards.
- Push through. You can keep going, even when it gets hard, knowing that it will pay off in great dividends if you lean into the dip.

When facing adversity, you have a choice: you can let up, or you can get ahead of everyone who chose to let up.

Profitable Pain

Ultramarathoning is a sport of enduring pain. You win by persevering when everyone else is quitting. Ultramarathoner Dick Collins said, "Decide before the race the conditions that will cause you to stop and drop out. You don't want to be out there saying, 'Well gee, my leg hurts, I'm a little dehydrated, I'm sleepy, I'm tired, and it's cold and windy.' And talk yourself into quitting. If you are making a decision based on how you feel in the moment, you will probably make the wrong decision." Ultramarathoners take embracing adversity to the next level. They know with almost certainty that during every race, they are going to come to a point where they want to quit. The only way to persevere when every muscle in your body is crying out for you to stop is to live by your commitments, not your feelings. When you live by your commitments, you outlast everyone else who quits when they hit the dip.

Just because it is unpleasant, does not mean it's unprofitable. When you avoid pain, you stay the same. You have to get sore to get strong. If you want to grow, if you want to change, embrace adversity–it's how you get better.

Ultramarathoner Dean Karnazes said, "Western culture has things a little backwards right now. We think that if we had every comfort available to us, we'd be happy. We equate comfort with happiness. And now, we're so comfortable we're miserable. There's no struggle in our lives. No sense of adventure. We get in a car, we get in an elevator, it all comes easy. What I've found is that I'm never more alive than when I'm pushing and I'm in pain, and I'm struggling for high achievement, and in that struggle I think there's a magic." Some of the greatest joy in life comes from going through adversity. In the struggle, we discover how strong we really are. You come out of the dip a changed person; that's the point of the dip.

"Of all the virtues we can learn, no trait is more useful, more essential to survival, and more likely to improve the quality of life than the ability to transform adversity into an enjoyable challenge."
- Mihaly Csikszentmihalyi

Quitting when it gets hard is human nature. When it hurts, our brains tell us to stop. Regardless of your level of fitness, at some point when you've done enough sprints, ran enough miles, or put up enough shots, your instincts are going to tell you to quit.

It's easy to start things. The gym is very crowded on January 1st and not so crowded on December 1st. When things get hard and there isn't as much visible progress, most people listen to that voice telling them to quit instead of the whisper telling them to keep going.

The offseason is the same way. There aren't game days where you can see your progress paying off. Days consist of monotonous strength and conditioning workouts, and thousands of unseen reps on the court. It's not very exciting or instantly gratifying, so most people quit.

Quitting doesn't necessarily mean you hang up your high-tops and decide to stop playing basketball. Another form of quitting is dialing back your level of commitment, exerting less effort, taking it easy, and ceasing to move forward.

The beginning is different. When we first begin doing something, the progress is a little more evident, it's interesting and exciting until the progress slows, the excitement lessens, it gets frustrating, practice gets a lot harder; it was great until you hit the dip.

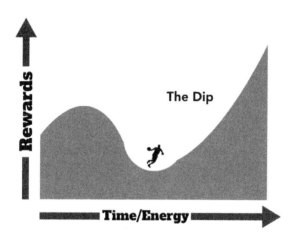

If you have ever been to a tryout, you know what the dip is. It's that hard drill or the tough conditioning test designed to weed out those who don't *really* want to be on the team. It is designed to make you want to quit.

"We are all faced with a series of great opportunities brilliantly disguised as impossible situations."
- Charles R. Swindoll

The dip is a system put into place to separate mediocre players from great players. There are lots of dips. The offseason is one big dip made up of a series of smaller dips. Once you are able to recognize the dips, you can see them for the opportunities they provide so you can work through them with the right mindset.

About halfway through any lift, practice, or drill, there comes a moment when it gets hard and frustrating. This comes when you don't see any results and it would be a lot more comfortable to go through the motions or quit altogether. That is the dip. If you can make the counterintuitive choice to go *even harder* for a little longer in those moments, you will see big rewards.

It can be tempting to invest less time and energy whenever it gets hard, but if you keep going, you will soon see a dramatic payoff. You will also see a dramatic separation between you and everyone else. Letting up when we hit the dip is so easy. We do it without even thinking about it. It is extremely rare for a person to have more enthusiasm, more effort, and more intensity when it gets hard. Almost *no one* does that, which is why the dip will make you so valuable. When it gets difficult, you have the opportunity to separate yourself. Rise earlier, stay later, and go harder.

Becoming A Shooter Is A Dip

Once upon a time, there was a 5'6 125-pound high school sophomore who had dreams of playing basketball in college. He lacked strength, so he still shot the ball from his waist.

His dad told him that if he wanted to play in college, he would need to get his shot up above his head. He worked on it all summer. He had to completely relearn how to shoot. It was a dip, a difficult endeavor that included a lack of immediate results and the desire to quit.

It was so difficult that his brother even remembers how hard that summer was just to witness, "It was tough for me to watch them in the backyard, late nights, a lot of hours on the day working on his shot. They broke it down to a point where he couldn't even shoot at all. He would be back there at times crying, not wanting to work on his game. He had to do it rep after rep after rep to a point where he was able to master it."

That undersized sophomore is named Stephen Curry, and he's widely known as the greatest shooter basketball has ever seen. What if, while he was crying in his backyard, he would've quit? Basketball wouldn't be the same today. There were thousands who probably lacked strength and tried to adjust their shot, the only difference is when they got to the dip, they quit.

Steph was not born a great shooter, he became the best shooter by enduring the dip. A lot of basketball players are not willing to entirely change their shot and shoot a ton of reps, which is why there is only 1 Steph Curry, but it's also why he's so valuable.

If becoming a shooter was easy, if there was no dip, the NBA would be full of shooters with more size and strength than Steph, and he wouldn't have a job. But because becoming a shooter is so hard that most quit in the dip, great shooters are scarce and so much more valuable. This is why Ben Simmons, whose only weakness is shooting, was taken #1 in the draft. It's okay that he's not a talented shooter because anyone *can* become a shooter, it's just a matter of practice and going through the dip.

They said the same thing about Kawhi Leonard, the reigning NBA Finals MVP. Kawhi shot 25% from 3 at San Diego State. But Kawhi, who has a reputation for his tireless work ethic, worked on his shot. He worked through the dip to become a great shooter, and as a result, he is shooting over 38% from 3 in his NBA career.

It's never a matter of who was born with a jump shot, no one was. Whoever can get through the dip can become a shooter, but only a few are willing. The difference between a mediocre player and a great player isn't natural talent; it's their ability to push through the times when everyone else gives up. Becoming a shooter is a very steep dip, which means it's extremely challenging but also extremely rewarding.

The Dip is Your Greatest Ally

The dip is the best thing that could possibly happen because it gives you a chance to separate yourself from the rest of the pack. The fact that your circumstances got difficult is a good thing, because while everyone else is slowing down, you understand this is just a dip, so you know to do the opposite of slow down.

The dip is your secret to success because while most will give in to the urge to let up or give up, you will push harder—all the greats do. Anytime practice gets hard, *you should be happy about it*; it means you have the opportunity to pull ahead. The more you lean into the dips, the more you separate yourself, and the harder it will be for your competition to catch up.

You have to see all adversity as an opportunity to pull ahead because most people see it as an invitation to quit. The harder it gets, the better chance you have of separating yourself from everyone else.

So when you're on your 12th sprint in practice, everyone else will start thinking about how tired they are, how bad their legs hurt, and they will stop or slow down. If you want to be the best, you'll love the 12th sprint. Because while everyone else is making the emotional decision to quit, you recognize this is just another dip, and you'll push harder, and because of that, you'll be the best.

When the season comes, it becomes obvious who embraced the dips and who gave in to the urge to quit. Each game comes with a series of dips: when you're down by 20, when the game goes to double overtime, or when the refs are making terrible calls. When most would be tempted to give up or ease up, it's a dip you must push through with an even greater determination.

All the great players don't just buckle down and grit their teeth to get through the dip, they see the *opportunity* the dip provides so they *lean in and embrace the challenge of the dip.* You will see extraordinary results if you can go even harder through the dip, if you quit you'll be average.

Clarify your vision

This goes back to Viktor Frankl's logotherapy. He made his patients define what they wanted. Doctor Frankl wanted them to have a project that would get them out of bed in the morning. He wanted them to have a project that needed them to take action every day. He made his patients have the mindset that if I don't get out of bed and work on this project, bad things will happen. No one quits a marathon on mile 25 or mile 1, most quit around mile 20. The beginning is exciting and the end is exhilarating, but the middle is where the race is won or lost in your mind, and it's where you find out what you're made of. You have to *always* be thinking about the vision you have for the future to keep you focused. The clearer the vision, the greater the quality of work. The stronger your *why* is, the harder it will be to quit. Know what you want, and live by your commitments, not your feelings.

Conclusion

Sports don't build character. Sports do provide you with a series of challenges, and if you have the right mindset, you can use that adversity to shape your character into a stronger, more empathetic, more resilient, more motivated, and wiser version of yourself.

Today is the most important day of your life because today is the only day that you can control. Yesterday is gone, and tomorrow is not promised. Don't wish the days away just because it's a tough season of life. Don't just try to get through the days. Have the mentality that *today is the day,* and make it count.

Adversity does not define you, what you do next does.

View yourself as a hero, not a victim.

Show up and clap for others, even when it's not your turn.

Find meaning in adversity.

Live a good story.

Know what you want.

Keep changing.

Take action.

Choose joy.

Chase excellence.

Build relationships.

Be far more committed to the future than the past.

Believe the best is yet to come.

Live in hope, not fear.

Make the dip your greatest ally.

Embrace adversity.

Do these things, and your story will inspire others to live a more meaningful life.

To read more, follow
@BallisPsych on social media
and check out our website:
BasketballisPsychology.com

Acknowledgments:

I had a hard time feeling like an imposter while I was writing this book. You would not be reading this book if I had tried to do it alone.

Special thanks to...

Kelsey Griess, Taylor LaRoche, and Ellie Talamantez for being my shoulders to cry on, for calling just to tell me how amazing I was for writing a book, for helping me take my mind off the stress and have fun, and for believing I could be an author before I even believed I could.

Kamie Fournier for reminding me every time I went through something hard that this was just another chapter in my book.

And to all my friends, family, and followers who supported me through this journey. I'm constantly overwhelmed with gratitude.

References:

Boll Weevil Monument | This is Alabama. (2017, September 6). [Video]. YouTube. https://www.youtube.com/watch?v=R4hJaKfprP4

Day, H. T. (2021). *It's not your turn: What to do while you're waiting for your breakthrough*. IVP.

Frankl, V. E., Winslade, W. J., & Kushner, H. S. (2006). *Man's Search for Meaning* (1st ed.). Beacon Press.

Godin, S. (2007). *The Dip: A Little Book That Teaches You When to Quit (and When to Stick)* (1St Edition). Portfolio.

Jones, K. (2019, April 8). *Billy Donovan: "I Was Depressed" After Winning Second National Title at Florida*. Sports Illustrated. https://www.si.com/nba/2019/04/08/billy-donovan-depressed-after-second-national-championship-title-florida-gators-win

Maria Millett, Michigan State University Extension. (2018, October 2). *Challenge your negative thoughts*. MSU Extension. https://www.canr.msu.edu/news/challenge_your_neg ative_thoughts#:%7E:text=90%20percent%20of%20t hese%20thoughts,focus%20and%20lots%20of%20pr actice.

Radford, B. (2011). *Does the Human Body Really Replace Itself Every 7 Years?* LiveScience.Com. https://www.livescience.com/33179-does-human-body-replace-cells-seven-years.html

Snyder, B. (2005). *Save The Cat! The Last Book on Screenwriting You'll Ever Need*. Michael Wiese Productions.

Wilson, T. (2020, June 26). *UW Health research study results show significant and alarming mental health impacts on school closures and sport cancellations*. Wisconsin High School Sports | Wisconsin Sports Network | WisSports.Net. https://www.wissports.net/news_article/show/111097 1

Printed in Great Britain
by Amazon